SEDLON ACCORDION METHOD
BOOK 1=A
(Introducing the Accordion)
by
J. H. SEDLON

© International Music Publications Ltd
First published in 1947 by Sam Fox Publishing Co.
International Music Publications Ltd is a Faber Music company
3 Queen Square, London WC1N 3AU
Printed in England by Caligraving Ltd

ISBN10: 0-571-52966-6
EAN13: 978-0-571-52966-7

To buy Faber Music publications or to find out about the full range of titles available,
please contact your local music retailer or Faber Music sales enquiries:

Faber Music Ltd, Burnt Mill, Elizabeth Way, Harlow, CM20 2HX England
Tel: +44(0)1279 82 89 82   Fax: +44(0)1279 82 89 83
sales@fabermusic.com   fabermusic.com

INTRODUCTION

The SEDLON ACCORDION METHOD, the most modern and complete accordion instruction book published, not only provides the pedagogically correct approach necessary to gain the greatest measure of accordionistic achievement, but also makes the study of the accordion a thoroughly delightful experience.

Book 1-A, which can be used for any size instrument, from 12 to 120 bass, takes the student rapidly through the fundamentals in a manner to establish self-confidence from the first lesson.

This Method presents a new and scientifically correct program for mastering finger technique, enabling the accordionist to acquire the brilliant technique of the professional player far more rapidly than by indiscriminate and haphazard practice.

Included also is an easily understood course in Keyboard Harmony and its adaptation in harmonizing melodies and playing effectively from piano and violin music.

Each book contains a series of carefully graded and edited solos embracing all forms of music from Swing-Boogie to the Classics.

The Sedlon Accordion Method, comprising eight books, enables the instructor to provide a complete program of correct technical and interpretative solo material which will develop the musical potentialities of the student more rapidly and to a higher degree of artistry than has ever before been possible.

Contents

The Correct Playing Position

Adjust the straps snugly to prevent the instrument from shifting when being played.

The left strap should be somewhat shorter than the right, placing the keyboard in an easy playing position.

The Sitting Position

Rest the weight of the accordion on the left knee. To support the instrument in a firm position, place the lower corner of the keyboard against the right thigh.

The Standing Position

Keep the head and shoulders erect. Balance the weight of the body equally on both feet.

The Keyboard
12 Bass Keyboard

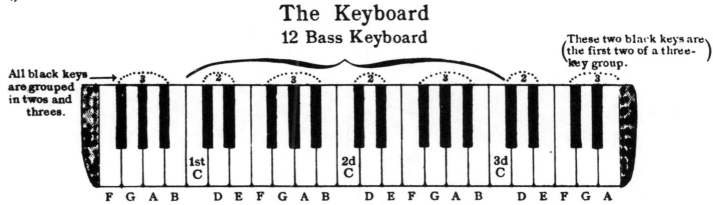

All black keys are grouped in twos and threes.

These two black keys are the first two of a three-key group.

F G A B   D E F G A B   D E F G A B   D E F G A

1st C   2d C   3d C

C is always the white key to the *left* of the *two* black-key group.

Notes to Play
The Whole Note

> The WHOLE NOTE ○ tells us one key is to be held down for FOUR COUNTS, **1 2 3 4**

Play the following whole notes on the keyboard with the Right Hand. Hold each one for 4 counts (or taps).

Memorize the Name of Each Note

Treble Clef Sign

Fingering

C D E F G F E D C

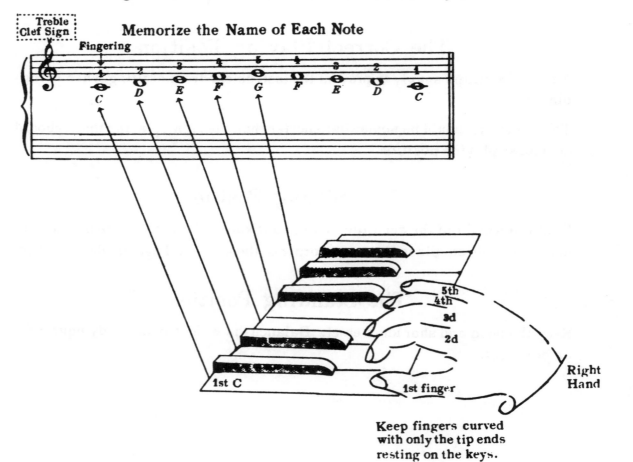

5th
4th
3d
2d
1st finger
1st C
Right Hand

Keep fingers curved with only the tip ends resting on the keys.

The HALF NOTE ♩ or ♩ is held for TWO COUNTS

The QUARTER NOTE ♩ or ♩ is held for ONE COUNT

Play and count (or tap)

Right Hand

Fingering 1 2 3 4 5 4 3 2 1

Fingering 1 2 3 4 5 4 3 2 1 5 1

The TIME SIGNATURE

The *upper* figure indicates the *number* of counts in each measure.

The *lower* figure indicates that a Quarter note gets *one count*.

Music is divided by BAR LINES into MEASURES.

1st Measure 2d Measure 3d Measure 4th Measure

Bass Clef Sign

Bar Line   Bar Line   Bar Line

For Reference
The WHOLE NOTE ○ : 4 counts.
The HALF NOTE ♩ : 2 counts.
The QUARTER NOTE ♩ : 1 count.

Merrily We Roll Along

Play slowly and evenly, observing the full time value of each note.

Fingering 3 2 1 2   3   2   3 5
Bellows out   Close   Out   Close

3 2 1   3   2 3   1
Out   Close   Out   Close

Locating the C and G Solo and Major Basses

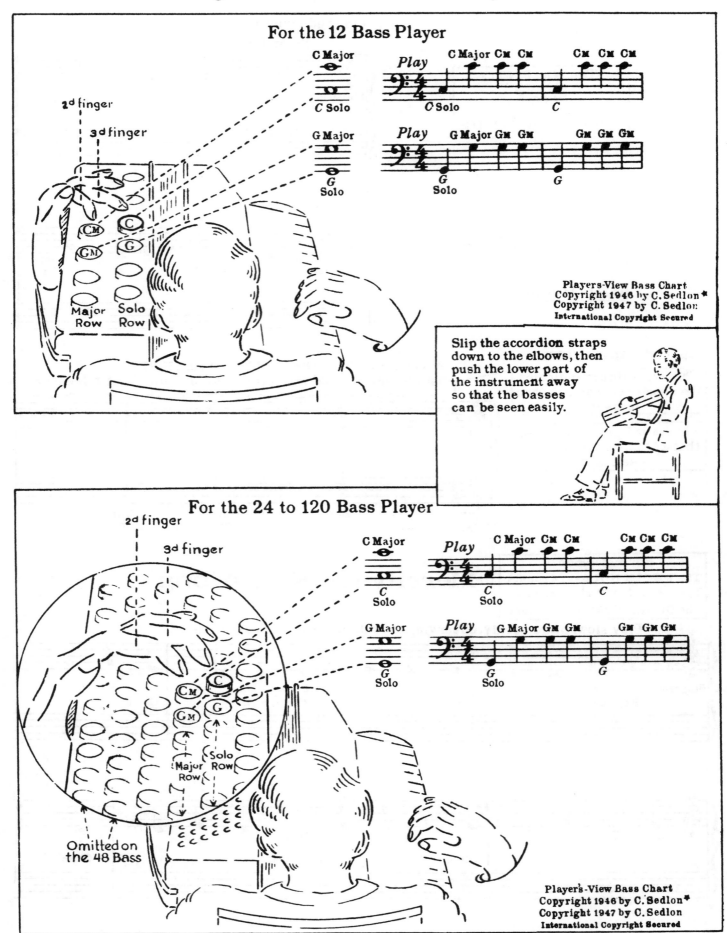

For the 12 Bass Player

Slip the accordion straps down to the elbows, then push the lower part of the instrument away so that the basses can be seen easily.

Players-View Bass Chart
Copyright 1946 by C. Sedlon *
Copyright 1947 by C. Sedlon
International Copyright Secured

For the 24 to 120 Bass Player

Players-View Bass Chart
Copyright 1946 by C. Sedlon *
Copyright 1947 by C. Sedlon
International Copyright Secured

The Basses

Return the accordion to the correct playing position and play the basses slowly and evenly.(see pg. 5)

Both Hands Together

Merrily We Roll Along

Note Review

Recite the letter names of the following notes: (do not play)

Preparatory Studies for the Right Hand

Deck the Halls

Brightly

Welsh Carol

Note Review

Name the kinds of notes following and give the number of counts for each:

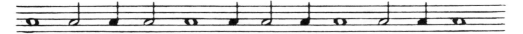

Locating the F Solo and Major Basses

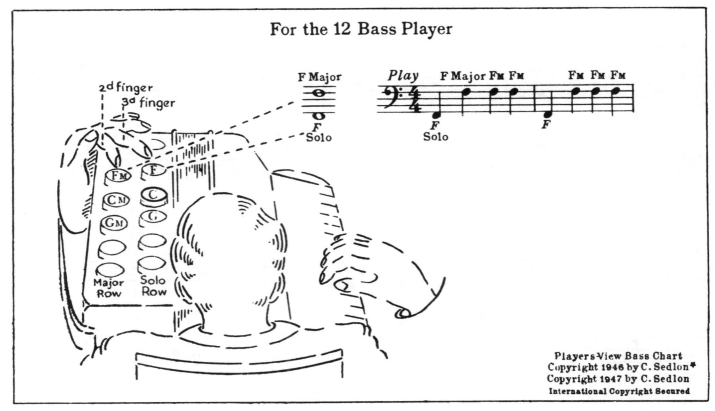

For the 12 Bass Player

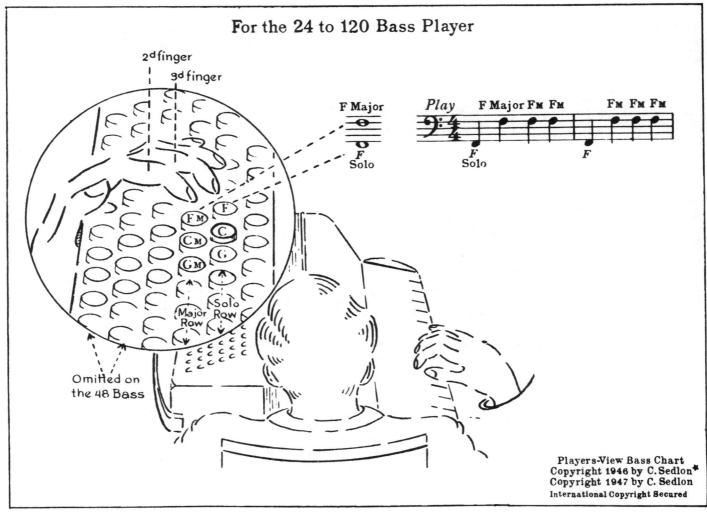

For the 24 to 120 Bass Player

* By permission of C. Sedlon

Bass Study

Jingle Bells

The Dotted-Half Note

The Dotted-Half Note 𝅗𝅥. or ♩. is held for three counts; the dot adds one-half the note's original time value. Thus, 𝅗𝅥 = 2 counts and 𝅗𝅥. = 2 + 1 or 3 counts.

The Waltz Bass

Cuckoo Waltz

Gracefully

Folk song

Little Village in the Mountains
WALTZ

Folk song

Moderato *(at a moderate rate of speed)*

The Sharp

The sharp ♯ *raises* a note one-half step.
Play F♯ on the black key to the *right* of the F.

Recite the letter names of the following notes: (do not play)

Locating the D Solo and Major Basses

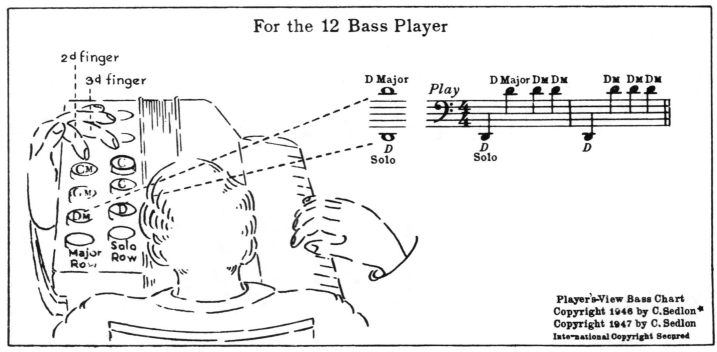

For the 12 Bass Player

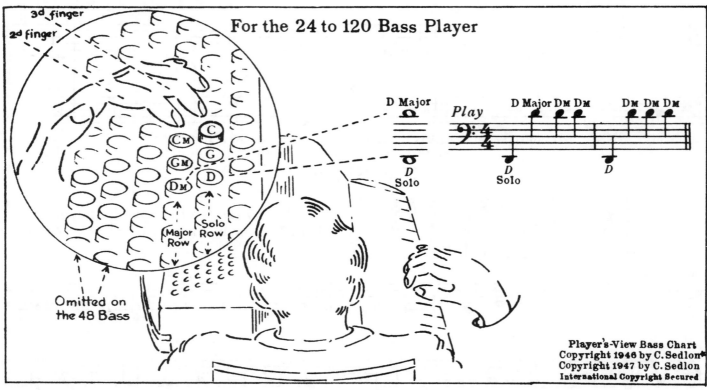

For the 24 to 120 Bass Player

Omitted on the 48 Bass

Bass Study

Playing in G Major

When F Sharp appears in the signature at the beginning of the staff, 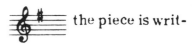 the piece is written in the key of G Major and all F's are played sharp throughout.

Serenade

Study in G Major

*The TIE: A curved line ⌢ or ⌣ connecting two notes on the same line or space is called a TIE. The second note is not struck but held for its full time value.

Reading Test

Recite the letter names of the following notes:

Phrasing

A curved line over a group of notes indicates a Phrase. Just as words are grouped into sentences, notes must be arranged in phrases to have meaning.

All notes within a phrase must be smoothly connected.

Lightly Row

Etude

Play smoothly and evenly

Au Clair de la Lune

Andante (*slowly*)

French Folk Song

Locating the B♭ Solo and Major Basses
(B Flat)

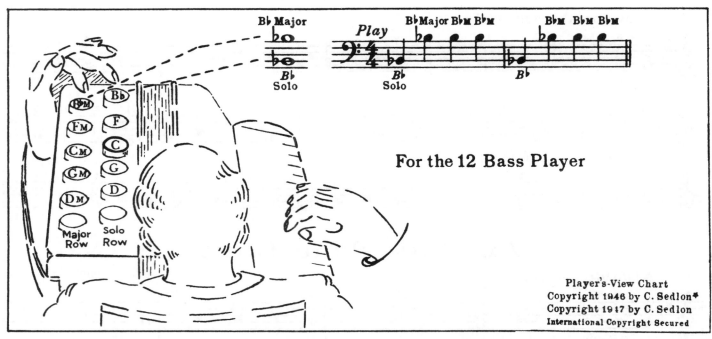

For the 12 Bass Player

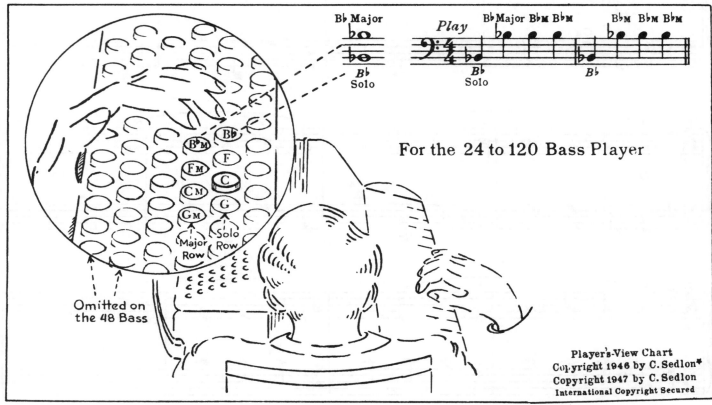

For the 24 to 120 Bass Player

Bass Study

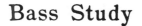

* By permission of C. Sedlon

The Flat

The Flat ♭ *lowers* a note one-half step.
Play B♭ on the black key to the *left* of B.

Playing in F Major

When **B-Flat** appears in the signature at the beginning of the staff, the piece is written in the key of F Major, and all B's are played flat throughout.

Twinkle, Twinkle, Little Star

Etude

Moderato

Long, Long, Ago

T. H. BAYLY

Etude

Smoothly, with a lilt

At the Village Inn
POLKA

Lively

Folk dance

Rests

Rests are signs of silence. No note is sounded for the time value of the rest.

Quarter Rest	Half Rest	Whole Rest
One Count	Two Counts	Four Counts

For He's a Jolly Good Fellow

Brightly

The Tie

The C Major Scale

Row, Row, Row Your Boat

Moderately fast

E. O. LYTE

Etude

Gracefully

Clog Dance

Folk Dance

Moderato

Etude

Smoothly and evenly

Peasant Dance
POLKA

Allegretto *(lively)*

Folk dance

29

The Alternating Bass

Evening Waltz

Folk song

Moderato

The G Major Scale

Come to the Sea

Folk song

Moderato

31

Etude

Mary in the Cabbage Patch
POLKA

Folk song

Three Blind Mice

Round

Allegretto

Comin' 'Round the Mountain

Brightly, with a swing

Folk song

Eighth Notes

An Eighth note ♪ is held half as long as a Quarter note. Play *two* eighth notes ♫ to *One Count*.

In counting time it will be easier to divide each count into halves: *for example*

Play and count

1 and 2 and 3 and 4 and   1 and 2 and 3 and 4 and   1 and 2 and 3 and 4 and

1 and 2 and 3 and 4 and | 1 and 2 and 3 and 4 and | 1 and 2 and 3 and 4 and | 1 and 2 and 3 and 4 and

Alouette

Moderato

French-Canadian Folk Song

At the Spring
WALTZ

Folk song

Two Etudes
in G Major

The Dotted-Quarter Note

♩. is held for one count and a half.

Silent Night

F. GRUBER

Tinker Polka

Animato

Folk dance

The small notes may be added at the teacher's discretion.

The F Major Scale

Oh My Darling Clementine

Slowly in a singing style

P. MONTROSE

Country Gardens

Moderato

Folk dance

The Jester

Folk Song

Moderato

Marela
POLKA

Allegretto

Folk dance

Locating the A Solo and Major Basses

For the 12 Bass Player

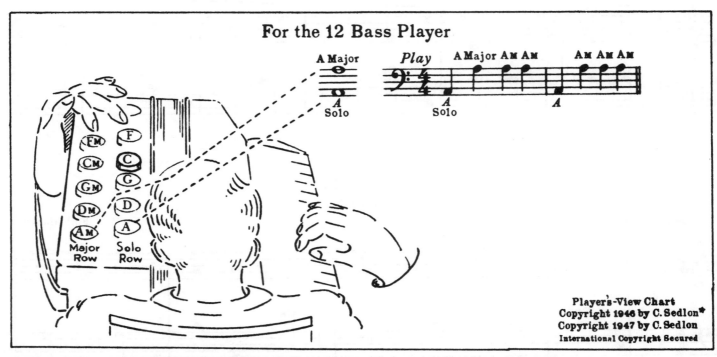

For the 24 to 120 Bass Player

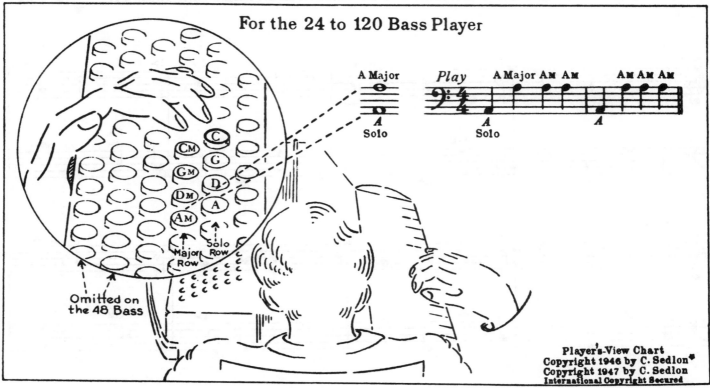

Bass Study

* By permission of C. Sedlon

The D Major Scale

Carnival of Venice

Moderato

44

The Minor Chord Row
(12 Bass Players omit)

Player's-View Chart
Copyright 1946 by C. Sedlon*
Copyright 1947 by C. Sedlon
International Copyright Secured

Minor Bass Study
(12 Bass Accordions omit)

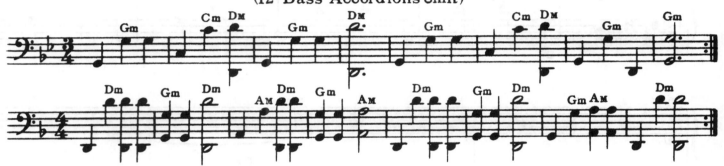

Farewell, Minka

* By permission of C. Sedlon

March Slav

P. I. TSCHAIKOWSKY

* C—Common time, same as $\frac{4}{4}$ Copyright MCMXLVII by Sam Fox Publishing Co., New York, N.Y.

Etude

Gracefully, with a swing

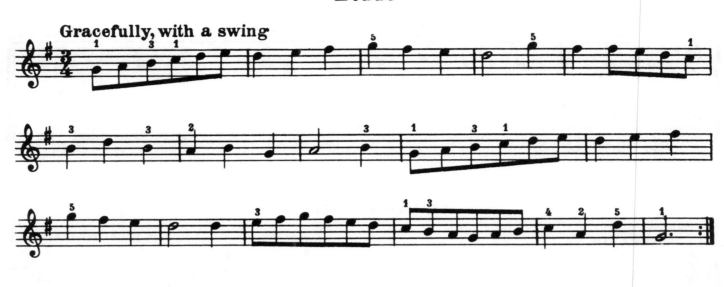

The Caissons Go Rolling Along

March time

* ¢ Alla Breve time. Two counts to the measure, a half note getting one count.

Upon completion of this book, proceed with the Intermediate Section,
Page 16, Book I-B of the Sedlon Accordion Method. (The first section
of Book I-B, pages 6-16, constitutes an optional review.)

GLOSSARY

Time Values of Notes

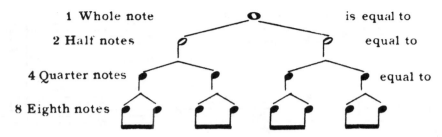

1 Whole note   is equal to
2 Half notes   equal to
4 Quarter notes   equal to
8 Eighth notes

Rest Signs; Rests are signs of silence. No tone is sounded for the time value of the rest.

Table of Rests and Notes of Corresponding Time Value

WHOLE REST equal in time value to a WHOLE NOTE	HALF REST equal in time value to a HALF NOTE	QUARTER REST equal in time value to a QUARTER NOTE	EIGHTH REST equal in time value to an EIGHTH NOTE

Time Signatures; At the beginning of each piece of music is indicated the number of beats there will be in each measure.

Four-four Time   Common Time   Cut Time(Alla Breve)   Three-four Time

4/4 same as   C   ¢   3/4
4 beats to each measure   4 beats to each measure   2 beats to each measure   3 beats to each measure

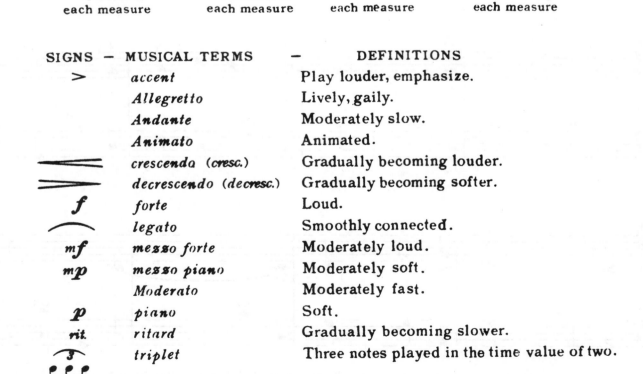

SIGNS	— MUSICAL TERMS	—	DEFINITIONS
>	accent		Play louder, emphasize.
	Allegretto		Lively, gaily.
	Andante		Moderately slow.
	Animato		Animated.
≤	crescendo (cresc.)		Gradually becoming louder.
≥	decrescendo (decresc.)		Gradually becoming softer.
f	forte		Loud.
⌒	legato		Smoothly connected.
mf	mezzo forte		Moderately loud.
mp	mezzo piano		Moderately soft.
	Moderato		Moderately fast.
p	piano		Soft.
rit.	ritard		Gradually becoming slower.
triplet sign	triplet		Three notes played in the time value of two.